THE SHIELD
OF A MUSLIM

THE SHIELD OF A MUSLIM

Said Osman

Editor: Stephen Zimmer

Published by Said Osman

ISBN Number: 9798871041352

Printed in the United States of America

First Edition

Table of Contents

Foreword

A shield is often defined as a broad piece of stout material, such as metal or wood, that is held using straps or a handle to one side of a person's body to use for protection against blows. However, it can also be defined as a person or something else that provides protection for an individual.

In this book, you will discover how supplications are important in that they are what helps to form a spiritual shield for a Muslim.

A supplication is an action that involves asking for something earnestly, and with humility. The Prophet Muhammad taught supplications for Muslims to recite as a form of worship, and these supplications also bring those who recite them many kinds of protections.

Supplications can bring protection to your home, the food that you eat, and your marriage. They can bring protection to you when you are traveling. They can bring you the protection that comes through consultation with Allah. They can also bring you protection from harmful creatures while you are sleeping.

Supplications are of the greatest importance in providing for you the kind of protection that you need in order to keep the things that negatively affect your life away.

Supplications are what makes the shield of a Muslim.

Introduction

When you look deep into Islam, you will see its beauty in everything that you do. With the remembrance of Allah and the way shown by the Prophet, everything turns into a form of worship.

Let's look at one example, which is the example of The Sleep. If you read all the supplications required from you, when you are sleeping, you are in a state of worship. That is why I want to remind myself and all Muslims, my brothers and sisters around the globe, by saying, "O Muslims, the environment around you isn't safe for you to go out without protection. Shield yourself with supplications taught by the Prophet. Your hidden enemies, Satan and his followers, don't want you to use your protection."

58:19 Al-Mujadila Qur'an "Satan has overcome them and made them forget the remembrance of Allah."

Every second, every minute, and every hour they are busy planning to harm you in every way possible, so don't be neglectful about your shield, and watch out for your enemies.

The Shield of A Muslim is a supplication book to guide Muslims to use their daily supplications to make a habit of using them until the end of their lifetime, to protect themselves from the hidden powers that try to harm them all the time. If they hold onto these supplications, they will be on the safe side with the help of Allah.

A soldier without a weapon can't fight. Don't let your enemies hunt you down and succeed in their evil planning. O Muslims, let's know that making a supplication is a form of obedience to Allah and our protection from any harm. That is why the Prophet said to not make your houses a graveyard, but read surah Al-baqarah in your houses, because Satan runs away from the house when surah Al-baqarah is read in it.

Sunan Abu Dawood 2044/ Sahih Muslim 780.

May Allah give us the understanding to understand His deen (religion) so that we can be beneficial and fruitful to the rest of mankind. May Allah open the doors of all goodness to anyone who reads this book, or spreads this message, or even looks into it, He is capable of everything.

The Importance of Supplication

Islam puts more importance on supplications because it is a way of getting closer to Allah and seeking His help in everything we do. When you turn the pages of the Qur'an, you will see Allah telling His servants that He is closer to them. So ask, and He will grant you whatever you ask of goodness.

"You alone we worship and you alone we ask for help" 1:5 Qur'an Al-fatiha.

This is a golden prayer given to us Muslims, in the beginning of the Qur'an, to communicate with Allah without any intermediary. O Muslims, worship Allah and run toward Him for help.

The Dua, or the supplication, is a great weapon

for the believer to use to solve all his problems and to present his needs to Allah, because all His doors are always open for acceptance. That is why when Yunus "As" cried for help and asked Allah for forgiveness, Allah opened the door of acceptance for him.

Allah also accepted the supplication of prophet Ayyub[Job].

وَأَيُّوبَ إِذْ نَادَىٰ رَبَّهُ أَنِّي مَسَّنِيَ الضُّرُّ وَأَنتَ أَرْحَمُ الرَّاحِمِينَ

"And [mention] Job, when he called to his Lord, "Indeed, adversity has touched me, and you are the Most Merciful of the merciful." 21:83 Al-Anbiya Qur'an Sahih International

فَاسْتَجَبْنَا لَهُ فَكَشَفْنَا مَا بِهِ مِن ضُرٍّ وَآتَيْنَاهُ أَهْلَهُ وَمِثْلَهُم مَّعَهُمْ رَحْمَةً مِّنْ عِندِنَا وَذِكْرَىٰ لِلْعَابِدِينَ

"So We responded to him and removed what afflicted him of adversity. And We gave him [back] his family and the like thereof with them as mercy from Us and a reminder for the worshippers [of Allah]." 21:84 Al-Anbiya Qur'an Sahih International

After Ayyub "As" made this special supplication, Allah cured him in a beautiful way, the way he mentioned it in chapter Saad, the thirty eighth chapter of the Qur'an. Allah says this about Ayyub [Job] in Sad verse 41-42

وَاذْكُرْ عَبْدَنَا أَيُّوبَ إِذْ نَادَى رَبَّهُ أَنِّي مَسَّنِيَ الشَّيْطَانُ بِنُصْبٍ وَعَذَابٍ

And remember Our servant Job, when he called to his Lord, "Indeed, Satan has touched me with hardship and torment." 38:41 Sad Qur'an Sahih International

ارْكُضْ بِرِجْلِكَ هَٰذَا مُغْتَسَلٌ بَارِدٌ وَشَرَابٌ

"[So he was told], 'Strike [the ground] with your foot; this is a [spring for] a cool bath and drink. 38:42 Sad Qur'an Sahih International

Yunus [Jonah] "As" left, going toward the sea after his people didn't listen to him out of disobedience. He left without giving a command to them, leading to him being thrown into the belly of the whale. Then, he cried to Allah from the darkness, admitting his mistakes. Then, Allah accepted his prayer, as we can see in the below verses from the noble book, The Qur'an.

وَذَا النُّونِ إِذ ذَّهَبَ مُغَاضِبًا فَظَنَّ أَن لَّن نَّقْدِرَ عَلَيْهِ فَنَادَى فِي الظُّلُمَاتِ أَن لَّا إِلَهَ إِلَّا أَنتَ سُبْحَانَكَ إِنِّي كُنتُ مِنَ الظَّالِمِينَ.

"And [mention] the man of the fish, when he went off in anger and thought that We would not decree [anything] upon him. And he called out within the darknesses, 'There is no deity except You; exalted are You. Indeed, I have been of the wrongdoers.'" 21:87 Al-Anbiya Qur'an Sahih International

When you raise your hands and make a supplication, the help of Allah and His protection isn't for the prophets only, but also for the righteous servants of Allah

فَاسْتَجَبْنَا لَهُ وَنَجَّيْنَاهُ مِنَ الْغَمِّ وَكَذَلِكَ نُنجِي الْمُؤْمِنِينَ.

"So We responded to him and saved him from the distress. And thus do We save the believers." 21:88 Al-Anbiya Qur'an Sahih International

The supplications are also to create a good environment for your progeny, for them to carry the message of Allah after you.

وَزَكَرِيَّا إِذْ نَادَى رَبَّهُ رَبِّ لَا تَذَرْنِي فَرْدًا وَأَنتَ خَيْرُ الْوَارِثِينَ.

"And [mention] Zechariah, when he called to his Lord, 'My Lord, do not leave me alone [with no heir], while you are the best of inheritors.'" 21:89 Al-Anbiya Qur'an Sahih International

Without any delay after the prophet Zechariah made the supplication to Allah, his supplication was accepted.

﴿ فَاسْتَجَبْنَا لَهُ وَوَهَبْنَا لَهُ يَحْيَىٰ وَأَصْلَحْنَا لَهُ زَوْجَهُ ۚ إِنَّهُمْ كَانُوا يُسَارِعُونَ فِي الْخَيْرَاتِ وَيَدْعُونَنَا رَغَبًا وَرَهَبًا ۖ وَكَانُوا لَنَا خَاشِعِينَ﴾

"So We responded to him, and We gave to him John, and amended for him his wife. Indeed, they used to hasten to good deeds and supplicate Us in hope and fear, and they were to Us humbly submissive." 21:90 Qur'an Al-Anbiya Sahih International

When you are in a-position of prostration, you

12

are more closer to Allah than anything else.

عَنْ أَبِي هُرَيْرَةَ أَنَّ رَسُولَ اللَّهِ صلى الله
عليه وسلم قَالَ « أَقْرَبُ مَا يَكُونُ الْعَبْدُ
مِنْ رَبِّهِ وَهُوَ سَاجِدٌ فَأَكْثِرُوا الدُّعَاءَ »
رواه مسلم

Abu Huraira reported:

"The Messenger of Allah (صلى الله عليه وسلم)
said: 'The nearest a servant comes to his Lord
is when he is prostrating himself, so make
supplication (in this state).'" Sahih Muslim 482

In this position of prostration, you humbled
yourself and lowered it by prostrating, so let's make
as many supplications as we can, because that is the
spot of humility. Say, "O Allah, you are the greatest
and solver of everything. To show us the importance
of supplications we are told a supplication is a way to
open the doors of Allah, and those who disdain his
worship will enter hellfire rendered as contemptible."

"And your Lord says, 'Call upon Me; I will

respond to you." Indeed, those who disdain My worship will enter Hell [rendered] contemptible."' 40:60 Chapter Ghafir Qur'an Sahih International

To conclude this chapter about the importance of supplication, make a habit of using all the supplications that you know, and learn new supplications for you to be under the protection of Allah.

When you use a supplication, Allah will teach you more and bless your days with protection and prosperity from places you can't imagine.

The House

When the light and the wisdom of faith from the mosques are brought into the houses and the people in the house start practicing the teachings of the mosque in their houses, those two lights will be connected and it will be hard to break them. That is why recitation of the Qur'an and the supplications causes a satan not to have any part of the activities going on in the house.

When you enter your house and you read the supplication taught by the Prophet upon entering the house, then your enemies will not have anywhere to stay or anything to eat for that night.

وعن جابر، رضى الله عنه قال: سمعت رسول الله صلى الله عليه وسلم يقول: "إذا دخل الرجل بيته، فذكر الله تعالى

عند دخوله وعند طعامه، قال الشيطان لأصحابه: لا مبيت لكم ولا عشاء، وإذا دخل ، فلم يذكر الله تعالى عند دخوله، قال الشيطان: أدركتم المبيت؛ وإذا لم يذكر الله تعالى عند طعامه قال: أدركتم المبيت والعشاء". ((رواه مسلم))

Jabir (May Allah be pleased with him) reported:

"I heard Messenger of Allah (صلى الله عليه وسلم)saying, 'If a person mentions the Name of Allah upon entering his house or eating, Satan says, addressing his followers: 'You will find no where to spend the night and no dinner.' But if he enters without mentioning the Name of Allah, Satan says (to his followers); 'You have found (a place) to spend the night in, and if he does not mention the Name of Allah at the time of eating, Satan says: 'You have found (a place) to spend the night in as well as food.'" [Sahih Muslim 2018].

My dear reader, may Allah have mercy upon you. Know that everywhere you go, you aren't safe. If your heart isn't connected to Allah, and remembering Him all the time, then Satan will have a share of everything you do, including your offspring. That is why we see children not obeying their parents and listening to the whispering of the Devil, to disobey their parents.

وَاسْتَفْزِزْ مَنِ اسْتَطَعْتَ مِنْهُمْ بِصَوْتِكَ وَأَجْلِبْ عَلَيْهِم بِخَيْلِكَ وَرَجِلِكَ وَشَارِكْهُمْ فِي

الْأَمْوَالِ وَالْأَوْلَادِ وَعِدْهُمْ وَمَا يَعِدُهُمُ الشَّيْطَانُ إِلَّا غُرُورًا.

"And incite [to senselessness] whoever you can among them with your voice and assault them with your horses and foot soldiers and become a partner in their wealth and their children and promise them." But Satan does not promise them except delusion. 17:64 Al-Isra Qur'an

Said Osman

Sahih International

وَشَارِكْهُمْ فِي الْأَمْوَالِ وَالْأَوْلاد

"And become a partner in their wealth and their children."

When you go and read the holy Qur'an, you will see the mother of Maryam (Mary) praying to Allah for her progeny to be protected from the whispers of the Devil.

﴿ فَلَمَّا وَضَعَتْهَا قَالَتْ رَبِّ إِنِّي وَضَعْتُهَا أُنثَىٰ وَاللَّهُ أَعْلَمُ بِمَا وَضَعَتْ وَلَيْسَ الذَّكَرُ كَالْأُنثَىٰ وَإِنِّي سَمَّيْتُهَا مَرْيَمَ وَإِنِّي أُعِيذُهَا بِكَ وَذُرِّيَّتَهَا مِنَ الشَّيْطَانِ الرَّجِيمِ ﴾

"But when she delivered her, she said, 'My Lord, I have delivered a female.' And Allah was most knowing of what she delivered, 'And the male is not like the female. And I have named her Mary, and I seek refuge for her in You and [for] her descendants from Satan, the expelled [from the mercy of Allah].'" 3:36 Al-Imran Qur'an Sahih International

The supplications of the parents are a great weapon to change the environment of a child and his future. The parents should pray to Allah wholeheartedly to make the future of their child bright, just like we can see in the Qur'an when "Zachariah" prayed to Allah to make Yahya [John] pleasing to his Lord.

وَإِنِّي خِفْتُ الْمَوَالِيَ مِن وَرَائِي وَكَانَتِ امْرَأَتِي عَاقِرًا فَهَبْ لِي مِن لَّدُنكَ وَلِيًّا

"And indeed, I fear the successors after me, and my wife has been barren, so give me from Yourself an heir." 19:5 Maryam Qur'an Sahih International

$$ يَرِثُنِي وَيَرِثُ مِنْ آلِ يَعْقُوبَ وَاجْعَلْهُ رَبِّ رَضِيًّا $$

"Who will inherit me and inherit from the family of Jacob. And make him, my Lord, pleasing [to You]." 19:6   Maryam Qur'an Sahih International

To show you the effect of the parents' supplications for their children, and training them to be connected to the creator, just go further down some verses in this same chapter. You will see that Allah accepted Zachariah Supplication and made Yahya a prophet.

After the supplications of John's father Zachariah, Allah sent blessings upon him, and he became dutiful to both his parents and he was given judgment at a young age.

$$ يَا يَحْيَى خُذِ الْكِتَابَ بِقُوَّةٍ وَآتَيْنَاهُ الْحُكْمَ صَبِيًّا $$

"[Allah] said, 'O John, take the Scripture with determination.'" And We gave him judgement [while yet] a boy.'" 19:12   Maryam Qur'an Sahih International

وَحَنَانًا مِّن لَّدُنَّا وَزَكَاةً وَكَانَ تَقِيًّا

"And affection from Us and purity, and he was fearing of Allah." 19:13 Maryam Qur'an Sahih International

وَبَرًّا بِوَالِدَيْهِ وَلَمْ يَكُن جَبَّارًا عَصِيًّا

"And dutiful to his parents, and he was not a disobedient tyrant."   19:14 Maryam Qur'an Sahih International

وَسَلامٌ عَلَيْهِ يَوْمَ وُلِدَ وَيَوْمَ يَمُوتُ وَيَوْمَ

يُبْعَثُ حَيًّا

"And peace be upon him the day he was born and the day he dies and the day he is raised alive." 19:15 Maryam Qur'an Sahih International

For the house and the household to be protected, it is important to make a supplication to Allah to make the house safe to live in.

Nuh[Noah] prayed to Allah, to make him settle in a good place that has blessings in it after having been saved with the Ark.

وَقُل رَّبِّ أَنزِلْنِي مُنزَلا مُّبَارَكًا وَأَنتَ خَيْرُ الْمُنزِلِينَ

"And say, 'My Lord, let me land at a blessed landing place, and You are the best to accommodate [us].' " 23:29 Al-Mu'minun Qur'an. Sahih International

The Prophet gave us a wonderful supplication

to read upon when coming to a place to live in. If you read it, nothing will harm you until you move out from that place.

عن خولة بنت حكيم رضي الله عنها قالت: سمعت رسول الله صلى الله عليه وسلم يقول: "من نزل منزلاً ثم قال: أعوذ بكلمات الله التامات من شر ما خلق: لم يضره شيء حتى يرتحل من منزله ذلك" ((رواه مسلم)).

Khaula bint Hakim Sulamiyya reported:

"I heard Allah's Messenger صلى الله عليه وسلم saying: When anyone lands at a place, and then says:" I seek refuge in the Perfect Word of Allah from the evil of what He has created," nothing would harm him until he marches from that stopping place." Sahih Muslim 2708

Dear reader, protection doesn't come overnight, but it needs continuous effort that doesn't stop. Put your trust in Allah and do the work needed from you by saying this supplication upon leaving your house, and upon your return.

عَنْ أَنَسِ بْنِ مَالِكٍ، قَالَ قَالَ رَسُولُ اللَّهِ صلى الله عليه وسلم " مَنْ قَالَ - يَعْنِي إِذَا خَرَجَ مِنْ بَيْتِهِ - بِسْمِ اللَّهِ تَوَكَّلْتُ عَلَى اللَّهِ لاَ حَوْلَ وَلاَ قُوَّةَ إِلاَّ بِاللَّهِ . يُقَالُ لَهُ كُفِيتَ وَوُقِيتَ . وَتَنَحَّى عَنْهُ الشَّيْطَانُ " . رواه الترمذي

Anas bin Malik narrated that the Messenger of Allah (صلى الله عليه وسلم) said:

"Whoever says – that is: when he leaves his house – 'In the Name of Allah, I place my trust in Allah, there is no might or power except by Allah (Bismillāh, tawakkaltu `alallāh, lā hawla wa lā quwwata illā billāh)' it will be said to him: 'You have been sufficed and protected,' and Shaitan will become distant from him.'" Sunan At-tirmidhi 3426

This is the supplication to be read upon entering

the house, for your entering of that house to be blessed.

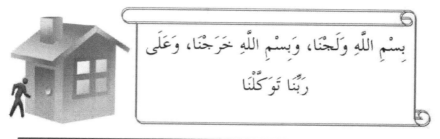

بِسْمِ اللَّهِ وَلَجْنَا، وَبِسْمِ اللَّهِ خَرَجْنَا، وَعَلَى رَبِّنَا تَوَكَّلْنَا

Bismillaahi walajnaa, wa bismillaahi kharajnaa, wa a'laa rab-binaa tawak-kalnaa.

In the name of Allah we enter, and in the name of Allah we leave, and upon our Lord we place our trust.*

This supplication is recorded in Sunan Abu Dawood 5096. For your information, dear reader, the great scholar Albani previously authenticated this hadith, then called it a weak narration because of a broken chain of narration between Shurayh ibn 'Ubayd, and Abu Malik al-Ash'ari.

Some scholars said this supplication isn't Sahih, or authentic, when it comes to the categorization of the hadith. Others have different opinions and say it is hasan, meaning good, like Sheikh ibn Baz, because they have proof from the noble Qur'an. The Qur'an says that when you go to someone's house, other than your house, to give them salam (greeting) without forgetting your family.

{ يَا أَيُّهَا الَّذِينَ آمَنُوا لَا تَدْخُلُوا بُيُوتًا غَيْرَ بُيُوتِكُمْ حَتَّىٰ تَسْتَأْنِسُوا وَتُسَلِّمُوا عَلَىٰ أَهْلِهَا ذَٰلِكُمْ خَيْرٌ لَّكُمْ لَعَلَّكُمْ تَذَكَّرُونَ }

"O you who have believed, do not enter houses other than your own houses until you ascertain welcome and greet their inhabitants. That is best for you; perhaps you will be reminded." 24:27 Nur Qur'an Sahih International

فَإِذَا دَخَلْتُم بُيُوتًا فَسَلِّمُوا عَلَىٰ أَنفُسِكُمْ تَحِيَّةً مِّنْ عِندِ اللَّهِ مُبَارَكَةً طَيِّبَةً كَذَٰلِكَ يُبَيِّنُ اللَّهُ لَكُمُ الْآيَاتِ لَعَلَّكُمْ تَعْقِلُونَ

"But when you enter houses, give greetings of peace upon each other - a greeting from Allah , blessed and good. Thus does Allah make clear to you the verses [of ordinance] that you may understand." 24:61 Nur Qur'an Sahih

International

عن أَنَسُ بْنُ مَالِكٍ قَالَ قَالَ لِي رَسُولُ
اللَّه صلى الله عليه وسلم "يَا بُنَيَّ إِذَا
دَخَلْتَ عَلَى أَهْلِكَ فَسَلِّمْ يَكُونُ بَرَكَةً
عَلَيْكَ وَعَلَى أَهْلِ بَيْتِكَ. رواه الترمذي

Narrated Anas:

"The Messenger of Allah صلى الله عليه وسلم said to me: 'O my little son! When you enter upon your family then give the Salam, it will be a blessing for you and upon the inhabitants of your house.'" Sunan at-Tirmidhi 2698

﴿ وَتَحْسَبُهُمْ أَيْقَاظًا وَهُمْ رُقُودٌ وَنُقَلِّبُهُمْ
ذَاتَ الْيَمِينِ وَذَاتَ الشِّمَالِ وَكَلْبُهُم بَاسِطٌ
ذِرَاعَيْهِ بِالْوَصِيدِ لَوِ اطَّلَعْتَ عَلَيْهِمْ لَوَلَّيْتَ
مِنْهُمْ فِرَارًا وَلَمُلِئْتَ مِنْهُمْ رُعْبًا ﴾

27

"And you would think them awake, while they were asleep. And We turned them to the right and to the left, while their dog stretched his forelegs at the entrance. If you had looked at them, you would have turned from them in flight and been filled by them with terror.: 18:18 Al-Kahf Qur'an Sahih International

These young men, who ran away for their faith in Allah, whenever they were sleeping, angels were turning them right and left.

Among the gifts given to our Prophet, one of them was short phrases, or words full of wisdom and showing good things about life. Let's stand upon one of the gifts given to our Prophet Muhammad that will lead us to see that sleep is a big blessing from Allah, The Almighty.

عَنْ حُذَيْفَةَ، قَالَ كَانَ النَّبِيُّ صلى الله عليه وسلم إِذَا أَوَى إِلَى فِرَاشِهِ قَالَ « اللَّهُمَّ بِاسْمِكَ أَحْيَا وَأَمُوتُ ». وَإِذَا أَصْبَحَ قَالَ « الْحَمْدُ لِلَّهِ الَّذِي أَحْيَانَا بَعْدَ مَا أَمَاتَنَا وَإِلَيْهِ النُّشُورُ ».

THE SHIELD OF A MUSLIM

Narrated Hudhaifah:

"When the Prophet (صلى الله عليه وسلم) went to bed, he used to say, 'Allahumma bismika ahya wa amut.' And when he woke up in the mornings he used to say, 'Al-hamdu li l-lahi al-ladhi ahyana ba'da ma amatana wa ilaihi-nnushur.' ("O Allah, In your name I live and die".) When he woke up he used to say, 'All praise is for Allah who gave us life after giving us death and unto him is the resurrection.'" Sahih al-Bukhari 7394

Let me present to you a few words full of wisdom, sweeter than the honey, heavier on the scale, full of rewards and brighter than anything you can imagine, better than all the gold and silver in the whole world.

اللَّهُمَّ خَلَقْتَ نَفْسِي وَأَنْتَ تَوَفَّاهَا
لَكَ مَمَاتُهَا وَمَحْيَاهَا إِنْ أَحْيَيْتَهَا
فَاحْفَظْهَا وَإِنْ أَمَتَّهَا فَاغْفِرْ لَهَا

Said Osman

" اللَّهُمَّ إِنِّي أَسْأَلُكَ الْعَافِيَةَ "

" 'O Allah, Thou created my being and it is for Thee to take it to its ultimate goal. And its death and life is due to Thee, and if Thou givest it life, safeguard it; and if Thou bringst death, grant it pardon. O Allah, I beg of Thee safety.'" Sahih Muslim 2712

When you go to sleep, read this amazing supplication, for it's a protection through the entire night and a good start to your morning activities.

اللَّهُمَّ أَسْلَمْتُ وَجْهِي إِلَيْكَ، وَفَوَّضْتُ أَمْرِي إِلَيْكَ، وَأَلْجَأْتُ ظَهْرِي إِلَيْكَ، رَغْبَةً وَرَهْبَةً إِلَيْكَ، لاَ مَلْجَأَ وَلاَ مَنْجَا مِنْكَ إِلاَّ إِلَيْكَ، اللَّهُمَّ آمَنْتُ بِكِتَابِكَ الَّذِي أَنْزَلْتَ، وَبِنَبِيِّكَ الَّذِي أَرْسَلْتَ.

("'O Allah! I surrender to You and entrust all my affairs to You and depend upon You for Your Blessings both with hope and fear of You. There is no fleeing from You, and there is no place of protection and safety except with You O Allah! I believe in Your Book (the Qur'an) which You have revealed and in Your Prophet (Muhammad) whom You have sent).'" Sahih Al-Bukhari 247

Anyone who reads this supplication and dies that night, dies with faith, as said by the Prophet of Allah.

To wake up and witness another day is a blessing from Allah, because sometimes you don't get the chance to see another day.

﴿ اللَّهُ يَتَوَفَّى الْأَنفُسَ حِينَ مَوْتِهَا وَالَّتِي لَمْ تَمُتْ فِي مَنَامِهَا فَيُمْسِكُ الَّتِي قَضَىٰ عَلَيْهَا الْمَوْتَ وَيُرْسِلُ الْأُخْرَىٰ إِلَىٰ أَجَلٍ مُّسَمًّى إِنَّ فِي ذَٰلِكَ لَآيَاتٍ لِّقَوْمٍ يَتَفَكَّرُونَ ﴾

"Allah, takes the souls at the time of their death,

and those that do not die [He takes] during their sleep. Then He keeps those for which He has decreed death and releases the others for a specified term. Indeed in that are signs for a people who give thought." 39:42 Az-zumar Qur'an Sahih International

To conclude, there are a lot of supplications to be read for your own protection before going to sleep that were taught by the Prophet. To learn more, it is better to dive in deeper into the supplication books like "Hisnul Muslim" (The Fortresses of A Muslim) by the great scholar Sa'id bin Ali bin wahf Al-Qahtani, born 1952 and died 2018, or Kitab Al-adhkar by scholar muhy al-Din yahya ibn sharaf an-nawawi.

The Consultation

Allah is the best planner of everything. Put all your affairs in His hands. Let him be your number one consultant, He will make the right decisions for you that you will not regret. That is why our beloved Prophet thought us how to submit all our affairs to Allah, for us to listen and for Him to guide us. As Musa "As" put all his affairs into the hands of Allah when he was looking somewhere to go, after running from pharaoh.

وَلَمَّا تَوَجَّهَ تِلْقَاءَ مَدْيَنَ قَالَ عَسَى رَبِّي أَن يَهْدِيَنِي سَوَاءَ السَّبِيلِ

"And when he directed himself toward Madyan, he said, 'Perhaps my Lord will guide me to the sound way.'" 28:22 Al-Qasas Qur'an

33

Sahih International

As the beloved of Allah, Prophet Musa put all his decisions into the hands of Allah for him to be rightly guided. Do the same thing and let Allah guide you too. Allah never lets His servant go astray, when He gives counsel to him about what is better for him in his life.

1 "As" may the peace of Allah be upon him.
The consultation is a command from Allah, because He knows what is better for each one of us. That is why he said in his noble book, the Qur'an:

$$\text{فَبِمَا رَحْمَةٍ مِّنَ اللَّهِ لِنتَ لَهُمْ وَلَوْ كُنتَ فَظًّا غَلِيظَ الْقَلْبِ لَانفَضُّوا مِنْ حَوْلِكَ فَاعْفُ عَنْهُمْ وَاسْتَغْفِرْ لَهُمْ وَشَاوِرْهُمْ فِي الْأَمْرِ فَإِذَا عَزَمْتَ فَتَوَكَّلْ عَلَى اللَّهِ إِنَّ اللَّهَ يُحِبُّ الْمُتَوَكِّلِينَ}$$

"So by mercy from Allah , [O Muhammad], you were lenient with them. And if you had been rude [in speech] and harsh in heart, they

would have disbanded from about you. So
pardon them and ask forgiveness for them
and consult them in the matter. And when you
have decided, then rely upon Allah . Indeed,
Allah loves those who rely [upon Him]." 3:159
Al- Imran Qur'an Sahih International

The golden supplication given to us from the
Prophet is below. Let's ponder upon it and benefit
from it, by memorizing and using it.

عَنْ جَابِرِ بْنِ عَبْدِ اللَّهِ ـ رضى الله
عنهما ـ قَالَ كَانَ رَسُولُ اللَّهِ صلى الله
عليه وسلم يُعَلِّمُنَا الاسْتِخَارَةَ فِي الأُمُورِ
كَمَا يُعَلِّمُنَا السُّورَةَ مِنَ الْقُرْآنِ يَقُولُ »
إِذَا هَمَّ أَحَدُكُمْ بِالأَمْرِ فَلْيَرْكَعْ رَكْعَتَيْنِ مِنْ
غَيْرِ الْفَرِيضَةِ ثُمَّ لِيَقُلِ اللَّهُمَّ إِنِّي أَسْتَخِيرُكَ
بِعِلْمِكَ وَأَسْتَقْدِرُكَ بِقُدْرَتِكَ، وَأَسْأَلُكَ مِنْ
فَضْلِكَ الْعَظِيمِ، فَإِنَّكَ تَقْدِرُ وَلاَ أَقْدِرُ
وَتَعْلَمُ وَلاَ أَعْلَمُ وَأَنْتَ عَلَّامُ الْغُيُوبِ،
اللَّهُمَّ إِنْ كُنْتَ تَعْلَمُ أَنَّ هَذَا الأَمْرَ خَيْرٌ لِي

35

فِي دِينِي وَمَعَاشِي وَعَاقِبَةِ أَمْرِي ـ أَوْ قَالَ عَاجِلِ أَمْرِي وَآجِلِهِ ـ فَاقْدُرْهُ لِي وَيَسِّرْهُ لِي ثُمَّ بَارِكْ لِي فِيهِ، وَإِنْ كُنْتَ تَعْلَمُ أَنَّ هَذَا الأَمْرَ شَرٌّ لِي فِي دِينِي وَمَعَاشِي وَعَاقِبَةِ أَمْرِي ـ أَوْ قَالَ فِي عَاجِلِ أَمْرِي وَآجِلِهِ ـ فَاصْرِفْهُ عَنِّي وَاصْرِفْنِي عَنْهُ، وَاقْدُرْ لِي الْخَيْرَ حَيْثُ كَانَ ثُمَّ أَرْضِنِي بِهِ ـ قَالَ ـ وَيُسَمِّي حَاجَتَهُ ».

Narrated Jabir bin `Abdullah:

"The Prophet (p.b.u.h) used to teach us the way of doing Istikhara (Istikhara means to ask Allah to guide one to the right sort of action concerning any job or a deed), in all matters as he taught us the Surah of the Qur'an. He said, 'If anyone of you thinks of doing any job he should offer a two rak`at prayer other than the compulsory ones and say (after the prayer):' -- 'Allahumma inni astakhiruka bi'ilmika, Wa astaqdiruka bi-qudratika, Wa as'alaka min fadlika Al-`azlm Fa-innaka taqdiru Wala aqdiru, Wa ta'lamu Wala a'lamu, Wa anta allamu l-ghuyub. Allahumma, in kunta ta'lam anna hadha-lamra Khairun li fi dini wa ma'ashi wa'aqibati `Amri (or ajilli `Amri wa'ajilihi) Faqdirhu wa yas-sirhu li thumma barik li Fihi, Wa in kunta ta'lamu anna hadha-lamra shar-run li fi dini wa ma'ashi wa'aqibati `Amri (or fi'ajili `Amri wa ajilihi) Fasrifhu anni was-rifni anhu. Waqdir li al-khaira haithu kana Thumma ardini bihi.' (O Allah! I ask guidance from Your knowledge, And Power from Your Might and I ask for Your great blessings. You are capable and I am not. You know and I do not and You know the unseen. O Allah! If You know that this job is good for my religion and my subsistence and in my Hereafter--(or said: If it is better for my present and later needs)-- Then You ordain it for me and make it easy for me to get, And then bless me in it, and if You know that this job is harmful to me In my religion and subsistence and in the Hereafter-- (or said: If it is worse for my present and later needs)--Then keep it away from me and let me be away from it. And ordain for me whatever

is good for me, and make me satisfied with it).'
The Prophet (صلى الله عليه وسلم)added that then
the person should name (mention) his need."
Sahih al-Bukhari 1166

"What we can learn from this supplication is
we don't know the outcome of our decision
we make in life so sit down and discuss all your
needs with Allah by saying you know what
is better but I don't so guide me and make
everything I want easy for me because what
you want sometimes isn't the best for you but
what the creator wants is best for you and he
will bring it in the best way on a better time."
2:216 Al-baqarah Qur'an Sahih International

وَعَسَىٰ أَن تَكْرَهُوا شَيْئًا وَهُوَ خَيْرٌ لَّكُمْ
وَعَسَىٰ أَن تُحِبُّوا شَيْئًا وَهُوَ شَرٌّ لَّكُمْ وَاللَّهُ
يَعْلَمُ وَأَنتُمْ لَا تَعْلَمُونَ

But perhaps you hate a thing, and it is good for
you; and perhaps you love a thing, and it is bad for

you. And Allah knows, while you know not.

Discuss with Allah and leave Him to make the decision for you, because he will not grant you something which will harm you.

فَسَقَىٰ لَهُمَا ثُمَّ تَوَلَّىٰ إِلَى الظِّلِّ فَقَالَ رَبِّ إِنِّي لِمَا أَنزَلْتَ إِلَيَّ مِنْ خَيْرٍ فَقِيرٌ

"So he watered [their flocks] for them; then he went back to the shade and said, 'My Lord, indeed I am, for whatever good You would send down to me, in need. '" 28:24 Al-Qasas Qur'an Sahih International

The consultation is very important in Islam, so let's practice to memorize this supplication and teach our children, to help them make better decisions in their life.

There is a complete chapter in the Qur'an called "Ash-Shura," meaning consultation, to show us how important consultation is in Islam, In that chapter, one of the true believer's signs is consultation.

Said Osman

42:38 Ash-shura Qur'an

وَأَمْرُهُمْ شُورَىٰ بَيْنَهُمْ

Who conduct their affairs by consultation:

When someone gives you a sound opinion, it's better to listen and put it into action. As narrated in the Qur'an, it can be about your safety.

وَجَاءَ رَجُلٌ مِّنْ أَقْصَى الْمَدِينَةِ يَسْعَىٰ قَالَ يَا مُوسَىٰ إِنَّ الْمَلَأَ يَأْتَمِرُونَ بِكَ لِيَقْتُلُوكَ فَاخْرُجْ إِنِّي لَكَ مِنَ النَّاصِحِينَ

"And a man came from the farthest end of the city, running. He said, 'Oh Moses, indeed the eminent ones are conferring over you [intending] to kill you, so leave [the city]; indeed I am to you one of the sincere advisors.'" 28:22 Al-Qasas Qur'an Sahih International

فَجَاءَتْهُ إِحْدَاهُمَا تَمْشِي عَلَى اسْتِحْيَاء
قَالَتْ إِنَّ أَبِي يَدْعُوكَ لِيَجْزِيَكَ أَجْرَ مَا
سَقَيْتَ لَنَا فَلَمَّا جَاءَهُ وَقَصَّ عَلَيْهِ الْقَصَصَ
قَالَ لَا تَخَفْ نَجَوْتَ مِنَ الْقَوْمِ الظَّالِمِينَ

"'Then one of the two women came to him walking with shyness. She said, 'Indeed, my father invites you that he may reward you for having watered for us.' So when he came to him and related to him the story, he said, 'Fear not. You have escaped from the wrongdoing people.'" 28:25 Al-Qasas Qur'an Sahih International

Musa "As" listened to the man who told him to leave the town because pharaoh and his people were trying to kill him. After he listened, Allah saved him from harm.

To conclude, consultation makes the person

respected and honored when he gives his/her opinion and others listen to it. It is a way to unite the hearts of all the people.

The importance of consultation was shown to us by putting it next to establishing the prayer, even though all the time, according to the Qur'anic verses after prayer, giving charity comes next.

The Traveling Supplication

Traveling is filled with opportunities for experience and wisdom. You can always learn something from traveling in life. Through traveling, you will gain a better understanding of other people's way of life, by sitting with them, and learning from them, about life from their own perspective. Traveling is encouraged in the Holy Qur'an in several different places, for us to learn something new from it.

أَفَلَمْ يَسِيرُوا فِي الْأَرْضِ فَتَكُونَ لَهُمْ قُلُوبٌ يَعْقِلُونَ بِهَا أَوْ آذَانٌ يَسْمَعُونَ بِهَا فَإِنَّهَا لَا تَعْمَى الْأَبْصَارُ وَلَكِن تَعْمَى الْقُلُوبُ الَّتِي

فِي الصُّدُورِ

"So have they not traveled through the earth and have hearts by which to reason and ears by which to hear? For indeed, it is not eyes that are blinded, but blinded are the hearts which are within the breasts." 22:46 Al-hajj Qur'an Sahih International

Before traveling, we have to pray for the safety of the family we are leaving behind, and for our safety, so that we can come back safe and sound.

Let me present to you this golden opportunity to teach you one of the Islamic treasures which is the supplication of traveling, which was taught to us by the Prophet in a caring way with loving words.

أَنَّ ابْنَ عُمَرَ عَلَّمَهُمْ أَنَّ رَسُولَ اللَّهِ صَلَّى اللَّهُ عَلَيْهِ وَسَلَّمَ كَانَ إِذَا اسْتَوَى عَلَى بَعِيرِهِ خَارِجًا إِلَى سَفَرٍ كَبَّرَ ثَلَاثًا ثُمَّ قَالَ سُبْحَانَ الَّذِي سَخَّرَ لَنَا هَذَا وَمَا كُنَّا لَهُ مُقْرِنِينَ وَإِنَّا إِلَى رَبِّنَا لَمُنْقَلِبُونَ

اللَّهُمَّ إِنَّا نَسْأَلُكَ فِي سَفَرِنَا هَذَا الْبِرَّ
وَالتَّقْوَى وَمِنْ الْعَمَلِ مَا تَرْضَى اللَّهُمَّ
هَوِّنْ عَلَيْنَا سَفَرَنَا هَذَا وَاطْوِ عَنَّا بُعْدَهُ
اللَّهُمَّ أَنْتَ الصَّاحِبُ فِي السَّفَرِ وَالْخَلِيفَةُ
فِي الْأَهْلِ اللَّهُمَّ إِنِّي أَعُوذُ بِكَ مِنْ وَعْثَاءِ
السَّفَرِ وَكَآبَةِ الْمَنْظَرِ وَسُوءِ الْمُنْقَلَبِ
فِي الْمَالِ وَالْأَهْلِ وَإِذَا رَجَعَ قَالَهُنَّ وَزَادَ
فِيهِنَّ آيِبُونَ تَائِبُونَ عَابِدُونَ لِرَبِّنَا
حَامِدُونَ

"Ibn Umar reported: 'When the Messenger of Allah, peace and blessings be upon him, would mount his camel for travel, he would exalt Allah three times and then say,' 'Glory be to Him who has made this subservient to us, for we have no power over it ourselves, and to our Lord we shall return. (43:14 Az-Zukhruf Qur'an) O Allah, we ask You during this journey for righteousness, fear of You, and deeds that are pleasing to You. O Allah, make this journey easy for us and make the distance short for us. O Allah, You are our companion during the journey and the guardian of the family. O Allah, I seek refuge in You from the hardship of travel, ugly scenes, and an evil return to our property and family.' When the Prophet returned, he would say these words and add to them, 'We are those who return, those who repent, those who worship and who praise our Lord.'"   Sahih Muslim 1342

In this golden supplication, Allah is teaching us to ask him to keep us safe, and those we left behind safe, by saying this: " O Allah we ask You during this journey for righteousness, fear of You, deeds that are pleasing to You. O Allah, make this journey easy for us. make the distance short for us. O Allah, You are our companion during the journey and the guardian of the family."

When we travel, we are concerned about those who we left behind, without forgetting our safety too. We don't know what is ahead of us, and that is why we need protection from everything harmful on our way.

The Eating

There is a big connection between what we eat and our actions. That is why it is commanded to eat what is lawful and good.

يَا أَيُّهَا الرُّسُلُ كُلُوا مِنَ الطَّيِّبَاتِ وَاعْمَلُوا صَالِحًا إِنِّي بِمَا تَعْمَلُونَ عَلِيمٌ

[Allah said], "O messengers, eat from the good foods and work righteousness. Indeed, I, of what you do, am Knowing." 23:51 Al-Muminun Qur'an Sahih International

If you eat something unlawful, it is hard for your supplication to be accepted, just as we can see from the sayings of the Prophet (Peace be upon him)

The Prophet (Peace be upon him) narrated to us about a man traveling who encountered some difficult hardships on his way. But Allah didn't accept his supplication, because of what he ate or what he was wearing, as we can see in Sahih Muslim.

عَنْ أَبِي هُرَيْرَةَ - رضي الله عنه - قَالَ: قَالَ رَسُولُ اللَّهِ - صلى الله عليه وسلم -: «إِنَّ اللَّهَ طَيِّبٌ لَا يَقْبَلُ إِلَّا طَيِّبًا، وَإِنَّ اللَّهَ أَمَرَ الْمُؤْمِنِينَ بِمَا أَمَرَ بِهِ الْمُرْسَلِينَ فَقَالَ تَعَالَى: «يَا أَيُّهَا الرُّسُلُ كُلُوا مِنَ الطَّيِّبَاتِ وَاعْمَلُوا صَالِحًا»، وَقَالَ تَعَالَى: «يَا أَيُّهَا الَّذِينَ آمَنُوا كُلُوا مِنْ طَيِّبَاتِ مَا رَزَقْنَاكُمْ» ثُمَّ ذَكَرَ الرَّجُلَ يُطِيلُ السَّفَرَ أَشْعَثَ أَغْبَرَ يَمُدُّ يَدَيْهِ إِلَى السَّمَاءِ: يَا رَبِّ! يَا رَبِّ! وَمَطْعَمُهُ حَرَامٌ، وَمَشْرَبُهُ حَرَامٌ، وَمَلْبَسُهُ حَرَامٌ، وَغُذِّيَ بِالْحَرَامِ، فَأَنَّى يُسْتَجَابُ لَهُ؟» رواه مسلم

Abu Huraira reported Allah's Messenger (صلى الله عليه وسلم) as saying

"O people, Allah is Good and He therefore, accepts only that which is good. And Allah commanded the believers as He commanded the Messengers by saying: 'O Messengers, eat of the good things, and do good deeds; verily I am aware of what you do.' (23:51 Qur'an) And He said: 'O those who believe, eat of the good things that We gave you.' (2: 172 Qur'an) He then made a mention of a person who travels widely, his hair disheveled and covered with dust. He lifts his hand towards the sky (and thus makes the supplication): 'O Lord, O Lord,' whereas his diet is unlawful, his drink is unlawful, and his clothes are unlawful and his nourishment is unlawful. How can then his supplication be accepted?'' Sahih Muslim 1015

يَا أَيُّهَا النَّاسُ كُلُواْ مِمَّا فِي الأَرْضِ حَلالاً طَيِّبًا وَلاَ تَتَّبِعُواْ خُطُوَاتِ الشَّيْطَانِ إِنَّهُ لَكُمْ عَدُوٌّ مُّبِينٌ

"O mankind, eat from whatever is on earth [that is] lawful and good and do not follow the footsteps of Satan. Indeed, he is to you a clear enemy." 2:168 Qur'an Al-Baqarah Sahih International

The love Allah had for His creation, and His care about them, is why He told them in His Book things which are unharmful and things which are harmful for them, for their own benefit. They should stay away from that which is harmful, like the swine, and the blood of some others.

حُرِّمَتْ عَلَيْكُمُ الْمَيْتَةُ وَالدَّمُ وَلَحْمُ الْخِنْزِيرِ وَمَا أُهِلَّ لِغَيْرِ اللَّهِ بِهِ وَالْمُنْخَنِقَةُ وَالْمَوْقُوذَةُ وَالْمُتَرَدِّيَةُ وَالنَّطِيحَةُ وَمَا أَكَلَ السَّبُعُ إِلاَّ مَا ذَكَّيْتُمْ وَمَا ذُبِحَ عَلَى النُّصُبِ

"Prohibited to you are dead animals, blood, the flesh of swine, and that which has been dedicated to other than Allah , and [those animals] killed by strangling or by a violent blow or by a head-long fall or by the goring of horns, and those from which a wild animal has eaten, except what you [are able to] slaughter [before its death], and those which are sacrificed on stone altars......" 5:3 Al-Ma'idah Qur'an Sahih International

If we want our supplications to be accepted, everything we eat should be permissible. We must do this so that the the actions we do will be welcomed in the sight of Allah.

The Marriage

Marriage is one the blessings the almighty God bestowed upon his creation since the beginning of the universe, beginning with Adam and Hawa.

The blessing of the marriage starts when you go out looking for the right spouse and the future mother of your kids.

For the blessing of the marriage to be achieved, Allah says this in his noble Qur'an, showing us the beauty of marriage.

سُوْرَةُ النَّبَإِ

بِسْمِ اللَّهِ الرَّحْمَنِ الرَّحِيمِ

وَخَلَقْنَاكُمْ أَزْوَاجًا ﴿٨﴾

"And We created you in pairs." 78:8 An-naba Qur'an. Sahih international

To further to show us the beauty of marriage and its blessing, this example of prophets have been used in the Qur'an of them having wives and kids.

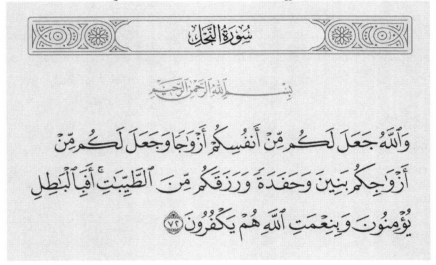

An-nahl 16:72 Qur'an Sahih International

"And Allah has made for you from yourselves mates and has made for you from your mates sons and grandchildren and has provided for you from the good things. Then in falsehood do they believe and in the favor of Allah they disbelieve?"

The creation of God keeps looking for enjoyment and happiness in life, so they were told that marriage has enjoyment if it is done to please the Creator.

وَمِنْ ءَايَـٰتِهِۦٓ أَنْ خَلَقَ لَكُم مِّنْ أَنفُسِكُمْ أَزْوَٰجًا لِّتَسْكُنُوٓا۟ إِلَيْهَا وَجَعَلَ بَيْنَكُم مَّوَدَّةً وَرَحْمَةً إِنَّ فِى ذَٰلِكَ لَـَٔايَـٰتٍ لِّقَوْمٍ يَتَفَكَّرُونَ ﴿٢١﴾

30:21 Ar-rum Qur'an Sahih international

"And one of His signs is that He created for you spouses from among yourselves so that you may find comfort in them. And He has placed between you compassion and mercy. Surely in this are signs for people reflect."

The beauty and the mercy of the marriage starts when its foundation of finding your spouse is correct and according to the laws of Islam. Then the beauty of the marriage and the happiness connected to it will be felt.

Marriage is not only about two people getting together, but also building a good environment to welcome children, for them to be fruitful to society. That is why Islam has a special supplication to be read during the meeting of the wife and the husband, as it prevents evil from going around the children and starting the whisper of the Devil.

Before anything else, the husband should follow this procedure with his wife, while holding his wife forehead and reading this supplication.

وعن ابن عباس رضي الله عنهما عن النبي صلى الله عليه وسلم قال: «لو أن أحدكم إذا أتى أهله قال: بسم الله، اللهم جنبنا الشيطان وجنب الشيطان ما رزقتنا، فقضى بينهما ولد لم يضره »

THE SHIELD OF A MUSLIM

((متفق عليه)).

Ibn 'Abbas (May Allah be pleased with them) reported:

''The Prophet (صلى الله عليه وسلم) said 'If anyone intends to have (sexual intercourse) with his wife, he should say: 'Bismillah! Allahumma janibnash-Shaitana, wa jannibish-Shaitana ma razaqtana (In the Name of Allah, O Allah! Keep us away from Satan and keep Satan away from what You have bestowed upon us); ' and if Allah has ordained a child for them, Satan will never harm him.''' Related by Sahih Bukhari 3271 and Sahih Muslim 1434.

The Qur'an presented a beautiful example of a mother making a-supplication to Allah on behalf of her child, for the child to be protected from Satan.

3:36 Qur'an

﴿ فَلَمَّا وَضَعَتْهَا قَالَتْ رَبِّ إِنِّي وَضَعْتُهَا أُنثَىٰ وَاللَّهُ أَعْلَمُ بِمَا وَضَعَتْ وَلَيْسَ الذَّكَرُ كَالْأُنثَىٰ وَإِنِّي سَمَّيْتُهَا مَرْيَمَ وَإِنِّي أُعِيذُهَا بِكَ وَذُرِّيَّتَهَا مِنَ الشَّيْطَانِ الرَّجِيمِ ﴾

"But when she delivered her, she said, 'My Lord, I have delivered a female. ' And Allah was most knowing of what she delivered, 'And the male is not like the female. And I have named her Mary, and I seek refuge for her in You and [for] her descendants from Satan, the expelled [from the mercy of Allah].'" Sahih international

To conclude this chapter, marriage won't be a successful one if its foundation isn't built with the laws and the orders of the almighty God. Marriage happiness will not be felt if both spouses didn't choose each other for the sake of faith.

As the beloved prophet of Allah, Prophet Muhammad, said in his sayings, the Hadith.

عن أبي هريرة رضي الله عنه، عن النبي صلى الله عليه وسلم قال: ((تُنكَح المرأة لأربع: لِمالها، ولحسَبِها، ولجمالها، ولدِينها، فاظفَرْ بذات الدين تربتْ يداك))؛ متفق عليه.

Abu Hurairah (May Allah be pleased with him) reported:

"The Prophet (صلى الله عليه وسلم) said, 'A woman is married for four things: for her wealth, for her lineage, for her beauty or for her piety. Select the pious, may you be blessed!!'" [Al-Bukhari 5090 and Muslim 1466].

Dear reader, every successful marriage is built upon understanding and good communication, after faith. So welcome your other half with an open heart and don't forget to read the supplication taught to us by the Prophet Muhammad before meeting your wife.

اللَّهُمَّ إِنِّي أَسْأَلُكَ خَيْرَهَا وَخَيْرَ مَا جَبَلْتَهَا
عَلَيْهِ وَأَعُوذُ بِكَ مِنْ شَرِّهَا وَمِنْ شَرِّ مَا
جَبَلْتَهَا عَلَيْهِ

"O Allah, I ask You for the good in her, and in the disposition You have given her; I take refuge in You from the evil in her, and in the disposition You have given her." Sunan Abi Dawud 2160.

Keep in mind that the marriage blessing comes into the marriage when the command of the Creator is fulfilled from the beginning of establishing the marriage, according to the Qur'an and the saying of the Prophet. This is the backbone of every success that can be achieved.

Marriage builds a beautiful society. Marriage shields the society from destruction caused by adultery that is why the truthful Prophet said the below phrase in the Islamic saying as encouragement to get married.

عَنْ عَبْدِاللَّهِ بْنِ مَسْعُودٍ رضي الله

عنه قَالَ لَنَا رَسُولُ اللَّهِ ﷺ يَا مَعْشَرَ
الشَّبَابِ، مَنِ اسْتَطَاعَ مِنْكُمُ الْبَاءَةَ
فَلْيَتَزَوَّجْ فَإِنَّهُ أَغَضُّ لِلْبَصَرِ، وَأَحْصَنُ
لِلْفَرْجِ، وَمَنْ لَمْ يَسْتَطِعْ فَعَلَيْهِ بِالصَّوْمِ؛
فَإِنَّهُ لَهُ وِجَاءٌ. مُتَّفَقٌ عَلَيْهِ.

Abdullah (b. Mas'ud) (Allah be pleased with him) reported that Allah's Messenger (صلى الله عليه وسلم) said to us:

"0 young men, those among you who can support a wife should marry, for it restrains eyes (from casting evil glances) and preserves one from immorality; but he who cannot afford It should observe fast for it is a means of controlling the sexual desire. Agreed upon Bukhari and Muslim." Sahih Muslim 1400C / Sahih Bukhari 5065

To conclude, marriage is a blessing from the Mighty One, to be established according to His command in order to have society progress in every aspect of life. Marriage is a door used to close off

Said Osman

every evil desire which comes in the way of mankind, like adultery.

The Conclusion

Every aspect of a Muslim life should have a connection with the Mighty One, the Creator of the universe, through His remembrance. In terms of establishing a new family or leaving your house, if you recite the supplications taught by the Prophet Muhammad, it will be for you a form of worship and you will be rewarded for that.

Before you sleep, if you do everything according to the ways of the Prophet, an angel will be appointed to protect you through your entire night from any harmful creature. Lastly, supplications are a way to show your love for Allah, who sustains and protects you from things you don't like to affect your life.

About the Author

Said Osman was born in Somalia state called Gedo. He went through different places for his Islamic knowledge. During his early childhood, he had a supporting family who helped him to join different madaris (Islamic School) for him to finish the Quran. Said is also a comparative religion student. At the moment, he is a teacher and Imam in his home city of Louisville, Kentucky.

Contact the author through his email:
Cajiinqas@gmail.com

,

Made in the USA
Columbia, SC
19 August 2024

40257682R20045